Happy Birthday Peggy

YOU

ARE A

SHINING

STAR

We LOVE You
leany Anne +

Sofia

Published by Sellers Publishing, Inc.

Copyright © 2019 Sellers Publishing, Inc.
All rights reserved.

Sellers Publishing, Inc.
161 John Roberts Road, South Portland, Maine 04106
Visit our Web site: www.sellerspublishing.com ● E-mail: rsp@rsvp.com

Designed by Mary L. Baldwin

Cover Illustration © 2019 Mia Charro/Jewel Branding Inc.

Interior image credits: pp. 4-5, 32-33, 62-63 © 2019 robert s/Shutterstock.com; pp. 8-9, 10-11, 26-27, 38-39, 40-41, 54-55 © 2019 white snow/Shutterstock.com; pp.14-15, 30-31, 44-45, 64 © 2019 suns07butterfly/Shutterstock.com; pp. 18-19, 22-23, 24-25, 46-47, 48-49 © 2019 Anatolii Vasilev/Shutterstock.com; pp. 20-21 © 2019 Yaroslav Vitkovskiy/Shutterstock.com; pp. 36-37, 42-43 © 2019 Zakharchuk/Shutterstock.com; pp. 56-57 © 2019 Ohishiapply/Shutterstock.com.

ISBN 13: 978-1-4162-4672-5

10 9 8 7 6 5 4 3 2 1

Printed in China.

YOU
ARE A
SHINING
STAR

BELIEVE IN YOUR JOURNEY

SELLERS
PUBLISHING

From the very start,

you set your sights

high above the

horizon.

No

dream

was too big

for your

boundless

imagination.

Dream big,
Sparkle more,
Shine bright.

UNKNOWN

No place was too distant

for you to explore.

No task was too daunting

or too scary for your

indomitable **spirit**.

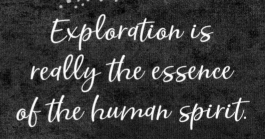

Exploration is
really the essence
of the human spirit.

FRANK BORMAN

With each

passing year,

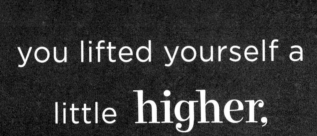

you lifted yourself a
little **higher,**

so determined,

so committed,

so passionate,

moving like a comet

towards your goal.

Your

journey

hasn't been an easy one.

Reach high, for stars
lie hidden in your soul,
dream deep for every
dream precedes the goal.

PAMELA VAULL STARR

There were times
when it took

everything
you had

to weather

the storms

you encountered.

There were
disappointments
and setbacks.

There were highs

and there

were lows.

Only when it is
dark enough, can you
see the stars.

MARTIN LUTHER KING JR.

But you persisted

through those

difficult moments.

If you feel like you don't fit into the world you inherited, it is because you were born to help create a new one.

ROSS CALIGIURI

You rose above your
doubts, and stayed

on course.

You kept **believing** in yourself and in your **dreams,**

When you follow a star . . .
it will guide you to where
you want to go. So it is with
the world. It will only ever
lead you back to yourself.

JEANETTE WINTERSON

and you found the

inner resources

to keep going.

Come on and shine,
Rising Star.

GAMMA RAY

You have traveled

past many **waypoints**

on your journey,

Set your course
by the stars, not by
the lights of every
passing ship.

OMAR N. BRADLEY

and had many

incredible

experiences

along the way.

Life is about
creating and living
experiences that are
worth sharing

STEVE JOBS

You have basked in the
golden light of the sun

and danced by

the silver light

of the moon.

You learned many lessons

and you made many friends.

*Keep your eyes on
the stars, and your
feet on the ground.*

THEODORE ROOSEVELT

And with each
new lesson,
each new experience,
each new friend,

you realized more

about yourself.

Your universe expanded

Don't wait for the stars
to align, reach up and
rearrange them the way
you want . . . create your
own constellation.

PHARRELL WILLIAMS

and your inner light

burned a little brighter.

*When you are joyful,
when you say yes to life
you become a sun in the
center of every constellation, and
people want to be near you.*

SHANNON L. ALDER

Now, your light

radiates outward

like an aura of color

inspiring those around you with its clarity, brilliance, and warmth.

Shine like the
whole universe
is yours.

RUMI

In the years to come, you will continue to ascend even **higher**.

You will accomplish

incredible things.

You will meet more **amazing** people.

Find a group of people who
challenge and inspire you, spend
a lot of time with them, and it
will change your life.

AMY POEHLER

You will help

make the world

a better place.

But now is a time

to **pause**,
to **reflect**,

to appreciate,
to celebrate

The more you celebrate
your life, the more there
is in life to celebrate.

OPRAH WINFREY

a **Shining** star,